GREEN DOG just woke up.
Oh no! He cannot remember
where he left his BONE!

He must visit his
favourite places to
solve the MYSTERY.

Did Green Dog leave his bone
at the place where
he caught a TRAIN?...

No, Green Dog did not leave his bone at the railway station.

Did Green Dog leave his bone where people sit inside a TIGER?

No, Green Dog did not leave his bone on the Tiger Tea bus.

Did Green Dog leave his bone where a man with BIG BOOTS sits in an OCTAGON?

No, Green Dog did
not leave his bone at the
Robert Burns statue.

ROBERT BURNS

Born 1759 in Ayrshire, Scotland,
he overcame poverty to become the National Poet of Scotland
and is remembered worldwide for his poetry and song, written in
Scots and English. Among his masterpieces are
"Auld Lang Syne", " A Red, Red Rose" and "Scots Wha Hae".
Robert Burns died in Dumfries in 1796.
His birthday is celebrated throughout the world by a Burns Supper.
Dunedin's first public sculpture, unveiled in 1887,
was funded by public subscription and sculpted by Sir John Steell (Edinburgh).
The poet's nephew, the Rev Thomas Burns, was a co-founder of
the Otago settlement (1848) and Presbyterian minister of Dunedin's First Church.
Dunedin Burns Club 2011

Did Green Dog leave his
bone behind when he slid
down a DINOSAUR?

No, Green Dog did not
leave his bone
at the Dinosaur slide.

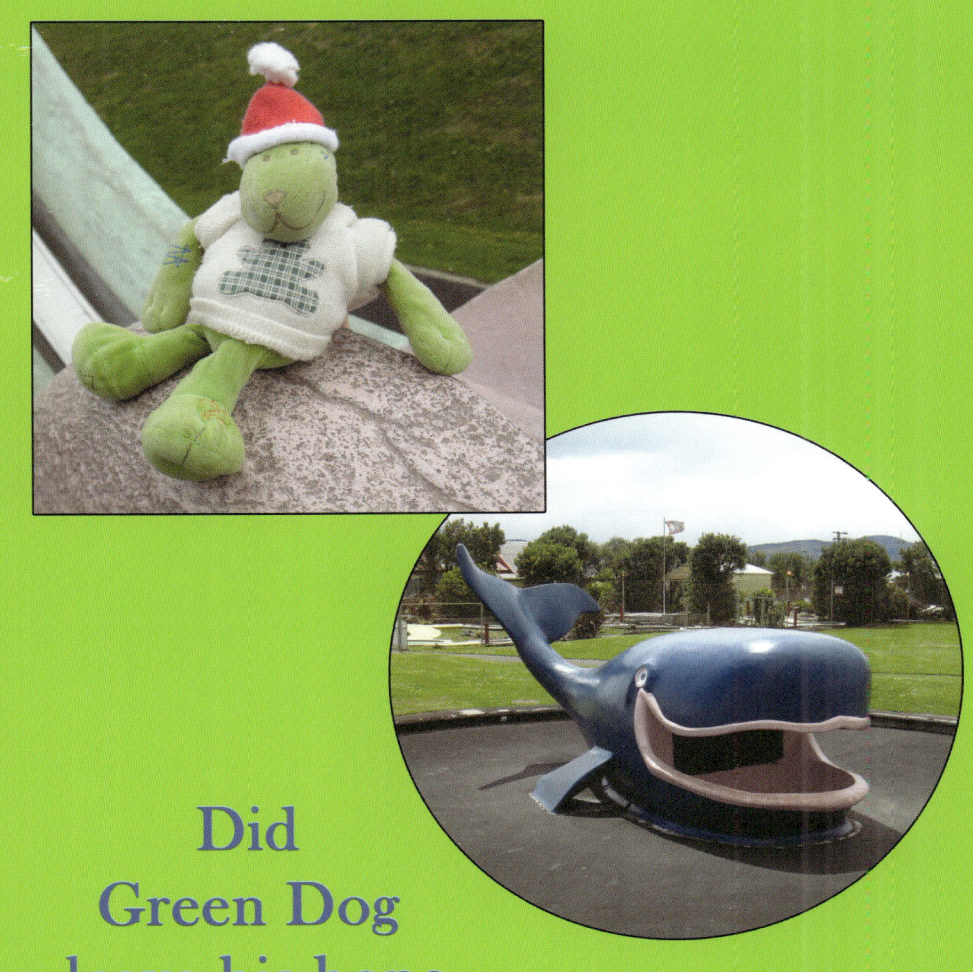

Did
Green Dog
leave his bone
on a SNOWY peak?

No, Green Dog did
not leave his bone on
"Mount Everest."

Did Green Dog
leave his bone
where the ocean
KISSES
the LAND?

No, Green Dog did not
leave his bone at
St. Clair Esplanade.

Did Green Dog
leave his bone
where ducks
STRIDE and QUACK?

No, Green Dog did not leave his bone at the duck pond. Where, oh where, can it be?

Did Green Dog leave his bone where animals are FROZEN in bronze?

No, Green Dog did not leave his bone at the Peter Pan statue.

Did someone put Green Dog's bone in a COLLECTION?

Green Dog says
"Those bones are not like mine!"

Green Dog has had a long day going
round and *round* the town.
It's time for bed!

Oh! There it is!

Green Dog's bone was under his PILLOW the whole time!

Yay! Now he can go to SLEEP and DREAM about his busy day.

THE END

Green Dog has some extra QUESTIONS for you:

Did you see a YELLOW bicycle?

Did you see an ORANGE balloon?

Did you see a man with BLUE shoes?

Did you see a CROOKED street lamp?

Did you see a photograph where Green Dog appears TWICE?

In how many pictures is Green Dog wearing his JERSEY?

In how many pictures is Green Dog wearing his HAT?

In how many pictures is there WATER?

How many WHALES appear in the book?

How many MINI Green Dogs appear in the book? Including this one:

Finally, how many of Green Dog's favourite places have YOU visited?

CPSIA information can be obtained at www.ICGtesting.com
Printed in the USA
BVIW12n2355070216
3759BVAU00005B/1